CHRISTMAS

Around The World

Scan & Review

Follow & Tag

camidesigncoloring

My Coloring Books

Different coloring pages for kids and adults.

Christmas Traditions From Around The World

Christmas is celebrated in many countries around the world. It all started over 2,000 years ago in a small town called Bethlehem when a baby named Jesus was born.

This event is the reason why people celebrate Christmas. The choice of December 25 as the date for Christmas is linked to the Roman Empire. In the 4th century, Christians in the Roman Empire began to celebrate the birth of Jesus on this date.

In some countries, there are very surprising ideas connected with Christmas, such as going to church on roller skates, decorating a boat, visiting KFC, keeping fish in the bathroom, or playing cricket. You will find the most interesting ones in this book!

We turned this book into a coloring adventure!

Make your own version of selected customs!
Try it out by scanning the code or
download free pages!

Color & learn!

CHRISTMAS
Around The World
Coloring Book

CHRISTMAS
Around The World
100+ festive traditions

Where can you spend Christmas at KFC?

Original **Christmas Traditions** to color!

Builds Empathy and Ap

cami designs

Buy a book   Get free pages

Beaches, cricket and Pavlova

G'day! One of Australia's most iconic Christmas traditions is celebrating under the summer sun. Christmas falls in the Australian summer, and many families head to the beach to enjoy the warm weather. It's a time for sunbathing, swimming, picnics, and beach games that create a very special Christmas atmosphere.

Australians often exchange presents on Christmas morning and children look forward to a visit from Santa Claus, who is known by the same name in Australia. Many Australian children set out a plate of cookies and a cold drink for Santa to enjoy during his visit.

Christmas decorations in Australia often include ornaments, lights, and tinsel. There are also typical Australian decorations, such as koalas, kangaroos, and other native creatures. Some families even decorate their homes with Australian plants such as eucalyptus branches and Christmas Bush.

A popular tradition is the "Carols by Candlelight" events that take place all over the country. These are outdoor concerts where people come together to sing Christmas carols by candlelight. Some of these Christmas events take place at symbolic and famous locations, such as the Royal Botanic Garden in Sydney.

Christmas Day is celebrated with a big feast, which often includes a "barbecue" or "BBQ" Families and friends prepare a delicious meal together. This meal can include sausages, seafood, and grilled meat.

Traditional Christmas desserts in Australia include the "Pavlova," a cake topped with fresh fruit, and the "Christmas pudding" However, due to the summer heat, some Australians opt for cold treats such as ice cream and fruit salad.

A quirky Australian custom is the "Christmas cricket match." On Christmas Day many families and groups of friends get together for a friendly game of cricket. It's a fun way to enjoy the great outdoors and work off some of the delicious festive food. Most people visit their friends on Boxing Day. This is a day when the annual sailing regatta from Sydney to Hobart, Tasmania, takes place.

In some parts of Australia, it's common to take part in "yabby races," where humans compete against small freshwater crabs called "yabbies".

Christmas in Australia is a time of outdoor adventures, beachside celebrations, and the joy of sharing unique customs with family and friends. It's a celebration that combines the spirit of Christmas with the sunny and warm Australian lifestyle, making it a truly special and heart-warming vacation.

Merry Christmas!

Brazil

Tropical Celebrations and Papai Noel

Olá! In Brazil, Christmas falls in the summer, which creates a warm and sunny atmosphere. Many people spend the holidays on the beach, enjoying the sun. It's the perfect time for picnics on the beach and outdoor fun.

One of the most popular Brazilian Christmas traditions is the "Amigo Secreto"," which means "secret friend." This is a festive gift exchange where friends and relatives draw names to exchange presents. The catch is that the identity of the giver remains secret until the gift is opened.

Brazilian homes are often decorated with colorful lights, ornaments, and Christmas trees. Although the traditional Christmas tree is very popular, in some areas of Brazil there are unique Christmas trees, such as the "Árvore de Natal Flutuante" or "Floating Christmas Tree" in Rio de Janeiro, a huge, illuminated structure that floats in the water.

The gift-bringer in Brazil is "Papai Noel,"

who is very similar to Santa Claus. He brings presents to the children on Christmas Eve, often dressed in a red suit and cap. The children eagerly await his arrival and lay out socks or shoes to receive their presents.

A beautiful tradition in Brazil is the "Ceia de Natal," a Christmas Eve meal where family and friends come together to celebrate with delicious food, music and dancing. The traditional Brazilian Christmas music, known as "Música de Natal," adds a special touch to the festivities.

For dessert, Brazilians enjoy a sweet treat called "rabanada," which is similar to French toast, as well as "bolos" or cakes and a variety of tropical fruits.

On Christmas Day, many Brazilians also attend church services, especially the "Missas do Galo" or "Rooster Mass," which often takes place at midnight on Christmas Eve.

Receiving the "13th salary" (double your regular salary for December) at the end of the year is a common practice in Brazil! The aim is to boost the economy in the run-up to Christmas. Many people don't even think that other countries don't do this, as it has been done for decades!

Feliz Natal!

Genna, Timket and field hockey

Selam! Christmas in Ethiopia, known as "Genna," is a beautiful and unique celebration deeply rooted in ancient traditions. People celebrate on January 7 according to the Julian calendar. The Ethiopian Orthodox Tewahedo Church plays a central role in the Christmas celebrations.

In the 43 days before Christmas, many people observe a unique Advent fast. It is called the "Fast of the Prophets" (Tsome Nebiyat) and begins on November 25. Only one vegan meal is eaten each day during this period.

During the "Genna" celebration people dressed in white gather in churches for special services that often last all night. Processions journey from one church to another. People sing Christian songs, pray, and read the Bible.

A special highlight of the Genna is the re-enactment of the birth of Jesus. Beautifully decorated models of the Holy Family are displayed, often set up in a small thatched hut. People sing and dance around the crib.

Ethiopian Christmas is a big and joyous

occasion, with various traditional dishes served. "Doro Wat," a spicy chicken stew, and "Injera," a flatbread made from sourdough, are some of the most popular dishes.

Ethiopian Christmas is also known for the unique tradition of "Timket" or Epiphany, which takes place on January 19. Timket is a colorful and lively celebration of the baptism of Jesus in the Jordan River. It includes a solemn re-enactment of the baptism with processions and the blessing of the water.

Christmas decorations in Ethiopia are simple. People often light candles and place them in the windows. No gifts are given or received during Genna and Timket. Children may receive only a small gift from the closest family members, e.g. a few items of clothing. It's more a time for eating and attending church.

In Ethiopia, there is an interesting tradition of playing field hockey during the Christmas season. The participation in this game is enormous, and anyone can join. The saying goes that in this game, there are no social privileges; skills are what matter.

Melkam Genna!

France

Père Noël
and sweets

Bonjour! In France, Christmas is celebrated with the arrival of "Père Noël," Santa Claus. Similar to Santa Claus in other countries, Père Noël brings presents to well-behaved children on Christmas Eve.

In some regions of the country, there is a dark figure accompanying him, known as Le Pere Fouettard. Pere decides whether certain children have been naughty or not. Letters written by children to Santa Claus, requesting specific gifts and assuring good behavior throughout the past year, do not go unnoticed. Adults have a duty to respond. Most often it is a greeting card with good wishes and the information that Santa has received the message.

Some kids provide food and drink for "Père Noël" and his faithful donkey. The donkey carries Père Noël from house to house, and the treats are a thank you to Santa and his faithful companion.

Christmas in France is all about delicious food. On Christmas Eve, families gather for a big "Réveillon" feast, which often includes oysters, foie gras, roast meat, and a wide selection of delicious desserts.

One of the most popular Christmas traditions in France is the Christmas

tree trunk, also known as "Bûche de Noël." This isn't an ordinary tree log, but a sweet, delicious cake that looks like a tree trunk. It's often made from chocolate and decorated with festive symbols such as holly leaves and berries. In some parts of France, it is a tradition to enjoy up to 13 desserts during the holidays. They symbolize the 12 apostles and Jesus. Christmas Eve dinner begins with a glass of champagne. Doesn't that sound fantastic?

On Christmas Eve, families often attend the "Midnight Mass," also known as "La Messe de Minuit." This is a special service that commemorates the birth of Jesus and is a meaningful way to start the Christmas celebrations.

Another enchanting French tradition is the "Crèche" or nativity scene. Families depict the birth of Jesus in a beautiful display of figures.

On January 6, also known as Three Kings' Day or Epiphany, a special tradition is observed in France. French families buy a "Galette des Rois", a unique cake in which a small porcelain object, the "ève", is hidden. The lucky person who discovers the "ève" in their cake is proclaimed king or queen for the day, puts on a fantasy crown, and gets to choose their royal counterpart.

Joyeux Noël!

Germany

Tannenbaum and Festive Markets

Guten Tag! As Christmas approaches, it is time for a special Advent calendar. It's like a countdown to Christmas. Every day you open a door or a window to discover a hidden surprise or treat. This increases the waiting!

One of the most popular German traditions is of course the Christmas tree, also known as the "Tannenbaum." The candles are lit On Christmas Eve, making a magical sight. It's important to mention that the Christmas tree actually comes from Germany.

Since the Middle Ages, it has spread to nearly every corner of the world. However, it's worth noting that in many countries (mostly due to climate and different plant life), the Christmas tree is a new, commercial tradition and has to be made from artificial materials.

Something out of a fairy tale - Christmas markets - can be found in cities

all over Germany. They're full of festive stalls selling handmade crafts, delicious food, and warm, spiced drinks such as mulled wine "Feuerzangenbowle."

One of the most charming parts of the German Christmas markets is the gingerbread house. These sweet and spicy gingerbread creations are beautifully decorated with icing and candy, and you can't only look at them, but eat them too!

In Germany, children eagerly await the arrival of the Christ Child on Christmas Eve. The Christ Child is often depicted as a golden-haired angelic figure who brings presents to well-behaved children. This tradition is very old and dates back to the 16th century.

On Christmas Eve, families get together for a festive meal. The meal includes roast goose, sausages, and potato salad. Afterward, it's time to exchange presents. Unlike in other countries, German children believe that presents are brought by the Christ Child, not Santa Claus.

Frohe Weihnachten!

Greece

Karavaki
and Kourabiedes

Kalimera! Greece is famous for special Christmas decorations, which are more popular than Christmas trees. We are talking about the "Karavaki," or Christmas boat. Small boats, often decorated with lights and ornaments, are placed in homes to symbolize a safe journey and a prosperous year. This tradition has its roots in old Greece's maritime history.

One of the most cheerful Greek Christmas traditions is the "Kalanda", the singing of Christmas carols. Children and adults go from house to house singing traditional Christmas carols and spreading good cheer. They often play musical instruments such as triangles and drums while singing and are rewarded by the house owners with small gifts or treats.

In Greek folklore, mischievous creatures called "Kallikantzari" emerge from their underground dwellings on Christmas Day and play tricks on people until Epiphany on January 6. They have a special fondness for going down the chimney, much like Santa Claus, and hiding in your house, ready to surprise you. The "Kallikantzari" are also known to do some unpleasant things, such as rearranging furniture and messing up open containers of food, which is very unpleasant.

On Christmas Eve, families in Greece attend "Midnight Mass", also known as "Christos Gennatai" After the service, people return home to enjoy a festive meal with family and friends. One of the most important dishes on the menu is "Christopsomo", or "Christ's bread." This is a special bread, often decorated with a cross, which is traditionally baked on Christmas Eve.

"Kourabiedes" are another popular treat during the Greek holidays. These are delicious butter cookies. They are often dusted with powdered sugar and sometimes also contain almonds. They are a popular sweet at Christmas time.

Another important tradition in Greece is "Saint Basil's Day" Saint Basil, or "Agios Vasilis", is celebrated on January 1st. On this day, a special bread called "Vasilopita" is baked, in which a coin is hidden. The person who finds the coin in their bread is said to have good luck for the coming year.

The festive season continues with the Feast of the Epiphany, which is celebrated on January 6. On this day, a priest blesses the water, and people often gather by the sea or rivers to take part in the blessing of the water.

Kala Christougenna!

Iceland

The Yule Lads and the Christmas Book Flood

Góðan daginn! In Iceland, Christmas is celebrated with a group of mischievous characters known as the "Yule Lads." These thirteen brothers are the descendants of Gryla, a fearsome troll, and her husband Leppaludi. The Yule Lads are not the typical kind and generous gift-givers, but play tricks on people and get up to all sorts of mischief.

Each Yule Lad has his own personality and a special character trait. For example, there is Stekkjarstaur (Sheep Chop), who bullies sheep, and Skyrjarmur (Skyr Eater), who has a penchant for the yoghurt-like dairy product skyr. The Christmas boys arrive in the town one by one thirteen days before Christmas, and the last one leaves on Christmas Day.

As Christmas approaches, Icelandic children place a shoe on the windowsill and the Yule Lads place small gifts in the shoes of good children, while naughty children receive potatoes or other fun things. This tradition adds a fun touch to the Christmas season.

Another popular Icelandic Christmas tradition is the "Jolabokaflod" or the

"Christmas book flood." This is a unique way to celebrate the Christmas season. Icelanders exchange books as gifts on Christmas Eve, and the evening is spent reading and enjoying their new books. Icelandic bookshops bring out a wealth of new releases in the months leading up to Christmas, making the country a paradise for book lovers.

The "Advent calendar" is also a cherished tradition in Iceland. This isn't a typical calendar with chocolates, but often contains 24 small gifts and treats that children can look forward to every day in the run-up to Christmas.

In Iceland, Christmas decorations are often decorated with candles and festive lights. The Advent and Christmas season is also celebrated by making "Advent wreaths" from evergreen branches, candles, and ornaments. Similar to Finland, cemeteries are often decorated with fairy lights at Christmas time.

On Christmas Day, many Icelanders attend church services and enjoy a special meal, which usually includes a roast leg of lamb. After the meal, they exchange gifts and spend a lot of time with family and friends.

Gleðileg jól!

Italy

La Befana and the Feast of Seven Fish

Ciao! In Italy, Christmas is celebrated with the help of a kind and magical witch called "La Befana." La Befana brings gifts and treats to children on the night of January 5, the eve of the Epiphany.

La Befana is an old woman with a long, crooked nose. She is dressed in old and dirty clothes. She flies on a broom, enters homes through the chimney, and leaves presents in a stocking. Children who want to please her should leave a tangerine, orange, or a glass of wine on the table before bedtime. Children are told that if they are not good, the witch Befana will put coal, ashes, onions, or garlic in their holiday socks.

The Three Wise Men told Befana about the birth of Jesus, but she didn't make it in time to greet him because she got lost. Since then, Befana, flying on a broom, leaves presents in every home where a child lives, just in case Jesus is there.

Christmas decorations are often simple and elegant, with lots of twinkling lights, candles, and beautiful ornaments. One of the most famous Italian decorations is the

"Poinsettia," or "Stella di Natale," which means Christmas Star.

In Italy, Christmas is also a time for feasting, and one of the most important traditions is the "Festa dei Sette Pesci" - The feast of the seven fish. The number seven is said to represent the seven sacraments and the days of creation. The menu for the Feast of the Seven Fishes includes dishes such as "baccalà" (salted cod), calamari, prawns, and of course delicious seafood pasta. It's a time to enjoy the bounty of the sea and spend time with family and friends.

Another popular tradition in Italy is the "Nativity Scene" or "Presepe." These are elaborate representations that recreate the scene of the birth of Jesus with figures and miniature landscapes. In many towns, there are living nativity scenes. People dress up as Mary, Joseph, and the shepherds to be part of the scene.

On the first day of Christmas, the families come together for another festive meal. This usually includes traditional dishes such as "panettone", a sweet bread, and "pandoro", a cake dusted with powdered sugar. These treats are often connected with a glass of sparkling wine.

Buon Natale!

Japan

KFC meal and illuminations

Konnichiwa! Although Christmas is not a national holiday in Japan, it is celebrated in a rather unique way. One of the most famous Christmas traditions in Japan is to enjoy a festive meal from KFC (Kentucky Fried Chicken). It may sound surprising, but ordering a "Christmas Party Barrel" from KFC is a cherished tradition for many Japanese families. The tradition began in the 1970s when a clever marketing campaign by KFC introduced the idea, and it has become so popular that reservations often have to be made well in advance.

Another beloved tradition is the indulgence of Christmas cake. In Japan, Christmas cakes are beautifully decorated and often feature whipped cream and strawberries. These cakes are available everywhere and are simply part of the Christmas season in many households.

Decorating the house with Christmas lights and decorations is also a cherished tradition in Japan. Many cities and towns are decorated with enchanting "illuminations" that offer impressive light shows. It is a

common custom to walk through these illuminated areas in the evening and create a magical atmosphere.

Although Christmas Eve is not used for family gatherings in Japan, it is considered a romantic holiday. Couples often celebrate with a special dinner, and it is a popular time for marriage proposals. It is even one of the most popular evenings to go out for dinner in Japan. In many ways, it is similar to Valentine's Day celebrations in the US and UK. Young couples like to go for romantic walks to see the Christmas lights.

Beethoven's Ninth Symphony, the last act of which is known as "Ode to Joy," is a particularly well-known piece of music in Japan during the holidays and at the end of the year.

Japanese children eagerly await the arrival of "Hoteiosho". He is sometimes described as a Japanese Santa Claus who brings presents to the children. In some regions of Japan, there are variations of this gift-bringing figure.

The Japanese New Year, known as "o shogatsu," is more like a traditional Christmas in the West. Families gather around the New Year to exchange greeting cards and enjoy a special meal. On Christmas Day itself, some families exchange gifts, but it is not as widely celebrated as in some other countries. The focus in Japan tends to be more on the festive atmosphere and enjoying time with loved ones.

Meri Kurisumasu!

Mexico

Pinatas
and Las Posadas

¡Hola! Christmas in Mexico is a magical time full of colors. One of the most fun and colorful traditions in Mexico is the "piñata." A "piñata" is a colorfully decorated, star shape usually made of paper and filled with candy and toys.

People gather blindfolded and take turns trying to break the "piñata" with a stick. When the "piñata" finally breaks open, everyone scrambles to collect the goodies that spill out. It's like a treasure hunt for candy!

In Mexico, Christmas lasts nine days, from December 16 to 24. This special time is called "Las Posadas," which means "the inns." It involves reenacting the journey of Mary and Joseph to Bethlehem to find an inn. Every evening, children and adults take part in a procession carrying figures of Mary and Joseph from house to house. At each house, they sing songs and ask for shelter. Finally, at the last house, they're invited to a great feast with food, music, and the breaking of piñatas. Christmas carols are called "villancicos."

In Mexico, families celebrate the holiday season with "nacimientos," elaborate Nativity scenes that begin on December 16. More characters are added over time. On Christmas Eve, baby Jesus is placed in the crib, later the Three Kings join. This tradition isn't just for homes. Many town centers in Mexico feature massive Nativity displays with animals and all the characters.

There are two other important days during the Christmas Season in Mexico. 12 December: Day of the Virgin of Guadalupe (Dia de la Virgin de Guadalupe) and 6 January: Three Kings Day (Dia de Los Tres Reyes Magos).

One of the most important symbols of Christmas in Mexico is the "poinsettia." It's considered a lucky charm and is often used for decorations.

On Christmas Eve, called "Nochebuena," families gather for a big feast. They enjoy traditional foods such as "tamales", "bacalao" (dried and salted cod) and "ponche", a warm fruit punch. For dessert, there is "rosca de reyes," a sweet bread in the shape of a ring in which a figure is often hidden. Whoever finds the figurine gets to host a special party on February 2, the "Día de la Candelaria"

And of course, Mexican children look forward to receiving presents from "El Niño Dios" (the Christ Child) on Christmas Eve, just like Santa Claus in other countries.

¡Feliz Navidad!

Netherlands

Sinterklaas and Wooden Shoes

Goedemorgen! In the Netherlands, Christmas is about a beloved figure called "Sinterklaas". He's often shown as a tall, wise man with a white beard, similar to Santa Claus but with bishop elements. The most exciting day of the Sinterklaas festival is December 5, the so-called "Sinterklaasavond."

On this evening, children eagerly await the arrival of Sinterklaas and his helpers, the so-called "Zwarte Peten" (Black Petes). Sinterklaas arrives on a steamboat from Spain. All the church bells in the area ring joyfully when Sinterklaas and the Petes step off the steamboat. Riding a white horse, Sinterklaas leads a procession through the town.

Sinterklaas gives presents to good children, but bad children will be put in sacks and sent to Spain by the Petes to learn good manners!

These days, a lot of people dislike using "Zwarte Pieten." This is due to the fact that it is considered racist for the helpers who dress up for this celebration to typically be

white people wearing black makeup. As a result, you will now see more "Sooty Piet/Roetpiet" - people who don't wear any makeup at all and just have soot and dirt smudges on their faces.

The children place their clogs, the so-called "klompen" or "schoenen" by the fireplace or window, together with carrots and hay for Sinterklaas' horse. In return, Sinterklaas fills the shoes with gifts and treats. Children often receive chocolate letters corresponding to the first letter of their name and eagerly unwrap these delicious treats.

Christmas itself is also celebrated in the Netherlands, but compared to the Sinterklaas festivities, it is a quieter celebration. Then families have a special meal with dishes such as turkey, roast pork, and traditional Dutch treats.

Dutch Christmas decorations are simple but beautiful: candles, lights, and ornaments decorate houses and streets. A lovely tradition is the "kerststerren" (paper, minimalistic poinsettias), which are often placed in the windows to create a warm and welcoming atmosphere.

Vrolijk Kerstfeest!

Norway

The Magic of Nisse and Julekurver

God morgen! In Norway, Christmas is called "Jul" and is one of the most eagerly awaited festivals of the year. The Christmas season officially begins on December 1st, and children count down the days with an "Advent calendar." Each day they open a door or window to find a small gift or treat, creating a sense of excitement and anticipation.

One of the most iconic figures of Norwegian Christmas is "Nisse," a mischievous and friendly gnome-like creature. In Sweden, Nisse is called Tomte. It is believed that Nisse looks after the farm and its animals. During the Christmas season, it is traditional to give Nisse a bowl of porridge with butter to ensure his goodwill.

A central tradition in Norway is "Advent" and the lighting of "Advent candles." Every Advent Sunday, a new candle is lit to count down the weeks until Christmas. This ritual is often accompanied by the singing of traditional Christmas carols.

Norwegian homes are beautifully decorated for Christmas: wreaths, candles, and colorful ornaments adorn windows and Christmas trees. The Christmas tree is a very important element of the Christmas season. A typical Christmas tree decoration in Norway consists of tiny paper baskets known as "Julekurver," which are fashioned like hearts. Some claim that they were invented in the 1860s by the writer Hans Christian Andersen!

One of the most important Norwegian Christmas traditions is "Lillejulaften," or "Little Christmas Eve." It is celebrated on December 23 and is a time when families come together and prepare for the grand celebration on Christmas Eve. Traditional Norwegian dishes such as "ribbe" (roast pork belly) and "lutefisk" (dried fish) are often enjoyed during this festive meal.

It seems that witches and evil spirits like to make themselves known on Christmas Eve. To get rid of them, Norwegians cleverly stow away their brooms, a preferred means of transportation for these mystical beings. To scare off the unwelcome guests, the men traditionally fire three shots from their rifles into the air.

Christmas Eve is the most important day of the Norwegian Christmas season. Norwegian children eagerly anticipate the arrival of "Julenissen," who is similar to Santa Claus and brings gifts to well-behaved children.

After dinner on Christmas Eve, many Norwegians attend a "Julegudstjeneste," a Christmas service, to celebrate the birth of Jesus.

God Jul!

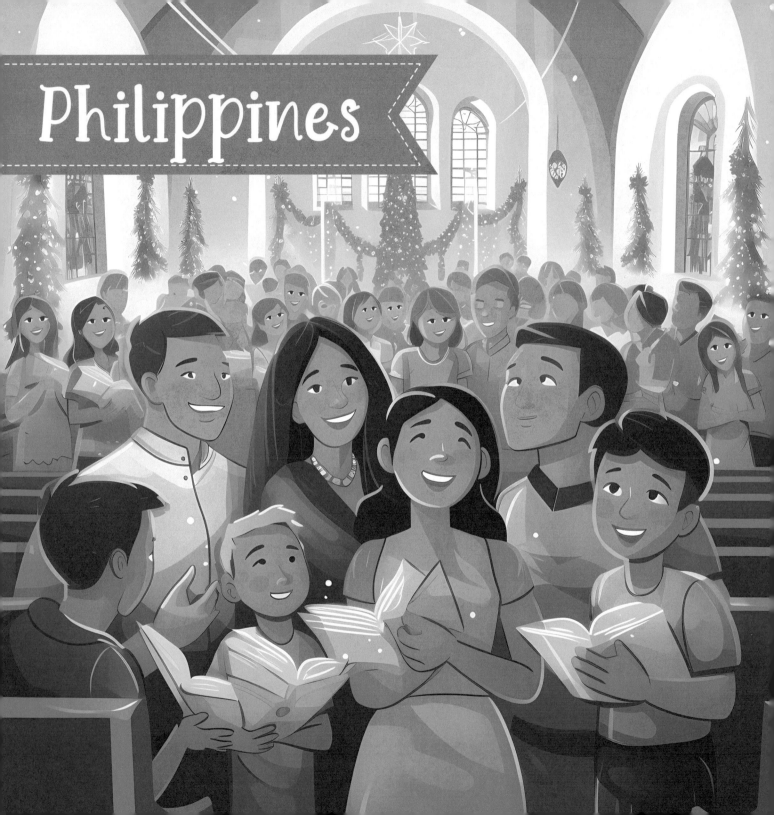

Philippines

Panunuluyan, Parol and Simbang Gabi

Kamusta! One of the most popular Christmas traditions is "Simbang Gabi," a series of nine masses before dawn that last until Christmas Eve. With this novena, Filipinos prepare themselves spiritually for the birth of Jesus. After each mass, people enjoy a variety of delicious Filipino dishes such as "bibingka" (rice cake) and "puto bumbong" (purple rice cake), which are often sold by street vendors outside the church.

Christmas decorations in the Philippines are colorful and extravagant. Houses, streets, and almost all buildings are decorated with blinking lights, ornaments, and other types of festive displays. In many cities, there are elaborate "belens" or Nativity scenes depicting the birth of Jesus with intricate figurines.

Another iconic Christmas symbol in the Philippines is the "parol", a traditional star-shaped lantern. Parols are in different sizes, from small ornaments to really giant lanterns that light up the night sky. They symbolize the Star of Bethlehem. Lantern-making competitions are held all over the country and communities come together to make these beautiful decorations.

On Christmas Eve, Filipino families come together for a big feast known as "Noche Buena," which often includes traditional dishes such as "lechon" (roast

pork), "hamon" (ham), and a wide selection of sweets and desserts.

A Filipino Christmas custom is the "Panunuluyan," which is a re-enactment of the Holy Family's search for shelter. People go from house to house looking for a place to stay while the residents pretend to turn them away. In the Philippines, carol singing is a popular activity where groups of carol singers visit homes, sing festive songs, and receive small gifts or money in return.

On 31 December, Filipino families gather for Media Noche ("Bisperas ng Bagong Taón"), a sumptuous midnight feast that, like Noche Buena on Christmas Eve, lasts until the next morning and is meant to symbolize hopes for future prosperity.

In addition to making noise to welcome the New Year, Filipinos also believe that the cacophony drives evil spirits from their surroundings. Despite the annual prohibition (caused by national government regulations), most towns and cities residents regularly light firecrackers.

Maligayang Pasko!

Opłatek, carp and pierogi

Cześć! In Poland, Advent heralds the Christmas season. It's a time full of peace, reflection, and a conscious effort to avoid excesses. Some attend special "Roraty" masses. In the days before Christmas, people do a big cleanup, wash the windows until they shine, and scrub the carpets super clean.

St. Nicholas' Day ("Mikołajki") is a cool holiday on December 6. Kids hope to score a little gift from "Small Nicholas," which is usually tucked into a shoe.

Before the great day, kids in schools and preschools perform "Jasełka" (Nativity Plays). This is a nice hit and often have a modern twist, sometimes making the Christmas story all modern and groovy.

Christmas Eve, known as "Wigilia," is one of the most popular holidays of the year. Families gather for a festive meal, but before the feast begins, a beautiful and heartwarming tradition takes place. It is a must to wear the best festive, elegant clothes on this ocassion. Many people visit hairdressers and beauticians to look good for Wigilia. As the sun sets on Christmas Eve and the first star appears in the sky - a symbol of the Star of Bethlehem - children and their families gather around the table. They will eat 12 different dishes (without meat). Each person holds a thin, rectangular wafer called an "opłatek." These

wafers are usually printed with religious scenes and patterns.

The tradition begins with the oldest member of the family taking a piece of opłatek and offering a small piece to the person on his or her right (and so on), along with wishes for health, happiness, and luck in the coming year. On this day, everyone tries to be nice. It happens that on Christmas Eve people forgive each other and try to reconcile.

After sharing the "opłatek", the Christmas Eve dinner begins with traditional dishes such as mushroom soup, pierogi (dumplings), fried carp, and various sweets ("makowiec", "sernik"). An important dish is "barszcz," a beet soup, and "bigos". Bigos is a traditional Polish stew made with sauerkraut and fresh cabbage, often containing a variety of meats and spices. You can eat "uszka" (small dumplings with mushrooms) or "krokiety" (pancakes with mushroom or cabbage filling, breaded).

The main course is often carp. People keep the carp in the bathtub for a few days before cooking it! Gifts are waiting under the Christmas tree and can only be opened after the meal. Naughty kids might find a "rózga," which is a dry twig.

At midnight, some people go to church and celebrate a mass called "Pasterka." Folks believe that when the clock strikes midnight, animals start chit-chatting. Christmas in Poland continues for two more days.

Wesołych Świąt!

Russia

Novogodnyaya Yolka and Ded Moroz

Priviet! In Russia, the main festival does not take place on December 25. The most important day is New Year's Eve. This is when "Ded Moroz" or Grandfather Frost and his granddaughter "Snegurochka", the Snow Maiden, bring presents to the children. Ded Moroz is similar to Santa Claus, but has his own story and appearance. He often wears a long, fur-trimmed coat.

On New Year's Eve, the children decorate a "yolka", a Christmas tree, with colorful ornaments and lights. Instead of putting the presents under the tree, they put them in a large bag or box. When the clock strikes midnight, Ded Moroz and Snegurochka come and give the presents to the excited children.

New Year's Eve, known as "Novogodnyaya Yolka", is a big celebration in Russia. Families come together to share a meal with traditional dishes such as potato salad, and "shashlik", a type of meat kebab. The highlight of the meal is often "blini", thin pancakes served with various toppings.

One of the most beautiful Russian Christmas traditions is the lighting of "yolka," which are birch branches decorated with colorful ribbons, apples, and other ornaments. These yolka are placed in the corners of rooms to symbolize the end of winter and the beginning of spring.

While Christmas itself is not a widely celebrated holiday in Russia, the

Russian Orthodox Church celebrates Christmas on January 7. It is a time for reflection on the birth of Jesus. Some people fast on Christmas Eve. This means that they abstain from certain foods. Until the first star appears in the sky. Then people eat "sochivo" or "kutia," a wheat or rice porridge flavored with honey, poppy seeds, chopped walnuts, fruit (especially berries and dried fruit such as raisins), and occasionally even fruit jelly! There are also Russian Christmas cookies called Kozulya. They are made in the shape of a sheep, goat, or deer.

„The Irony of Fate" (Ирония судьбы or Ironiya sudby) is a well-known and „traditional" film shown on television on New Year's Eve. It was recorded in 1975 during the Soviet era and broadcast on Soviet television on every New Year's Eve. It is also known as "Enjoy your Bath" or "With a Light Steam" In this romantic comedy, a man goes to the sauna with some of his friends and drinks too much, getting very lost.

S Rozhdestvom!

Braai
and Beaches

Sawubona! As South Africa is in the southern hemisphere, Christmas falls in the summer, making it the perfect time for a beach holiday. Many families spend the day on the stunning South African coast enjoying the sun, sand, and surf.

December 25, families across the country are filled with cries of joy and shouts of "Wake up, wake up! It's Christmas!" in many different languages. People gather under the tree, unwrap gorgeously dressed presents and share their love for one another. Church services are held in the morning, with many dressed in traditional costumes.

One of the most popular South African Christmas traditions is the barbecue "Braai." It's a way to celebrate the holiday. Families and friends gather outdoors and barbecue delicious meats such as lamb, boerewors (sausages), and steak. It's a time for outdoor sports, meals, picnics, and enjoying the warm summer, sunny weather. It is also popular to go for camping.

Although South Africa has a diverse population with different cultural backgrounds, Christmas traditions often incorporate elements from European and American celebrations. Santa Claus, is a popular figure who brings presents to the children.

Many South Africans take part in "Carols by Candlelight" events, where people sing Christmas carols under the night sky with candles in hand. These events are often linked to charity campaigns.

The Christmas table often features mince pies and Christmas pudding as well as other traditional dishes. But because of the summer heat, many South Africans also enjoy refreshing and tropical fruits such as watermelons and mangoes.

Ukhisimusi Omuhle!

Spain

Three Wise Men and El Gordo

¡Hola! One of the most exciting traditions in Spain is the "El Gordo" or "The Fat One." It's one of the largest lotteries in the world. The draw takes place on December 22, causing excitement and anticipation in households across the country. Winning El Gordo can be life-changing.

The real highlight of the Spanish festive season is the feast of "Los Reyes Magos," the Three Wise Men, on January 6. This day is known as "El Día de Reyes" (Epiphany Day) and is the day on which Spanish children receive their presents.

In the days leading up to Epiphany, parades take place throughout Spain with colorful floats and costumed performers representing the Three Kings and many other popular figures. The kings throw sweets and small gifts into the crowd and the children eagerly collect these treasures.

On the night of January 5, the children

prepare their shoes for the kings, so that they can fill them with gifts. They may also put a few treats for the kings and some hay or grass for their camels.

One of the most important Spanish Christmas traditions is the "Nativity scene" or "Belén." In families, the birth of Jesus is artfully portrayed, often with figures of Mary, Joseph, the shepherds, and the animals. Some "Belén" scenes are very elaborate and can even involve entire villages.

Christmas dinner in Spain often consists of a variety of delicious dishes such as "turron", a sweet nougat made from almonds and honey, and "roscón de reyes", a round cake decorated with candied fruit and often containing hidden surprises.

December 28 is known as "Día de los santos inocentes," or the "Day of the Innocent Saints," which is a kind of April Fools' Day in the United States and the United Kingdom. Individuals attempt to fool one another into accepting absurd jokes and stories. Silly stories are also on TV stations and newspapers. You can call someone "inocente, inocente," which translates to "innocent, innocent," if you trick them.

¡Feliz Navidad!

Sweden

St. Lucia's Day and the Tomte

God morgon! One of the most popular traditions in Sweden is the celebration of St. Lucia's Day on December 13. St. Lucia is a symbol of light and hope in the dark winter months. On this day, a girl is chosen to represent St. Lucia, wears a crown of candles on her head. She leads a procession of other children, singing traditional songs and offering saffron buns and ginger cookies.

In Sweden, Christmas is also a time when children eagerly await the arrival of the "Tomte, " a mischievous, gnome-like creature who brings gifts. It is believed that the "Tomte" lives on farms and protects all the animals. The children place a bowl of porridge in front of the "Tomte" to secure their goodwill and receive gifts in return.

Giving gifts has its origins in the tradition of "Julklapp," which means "Christmas knock." Many years ago, it was customary to knock on the door of a friend or neighbor and then leave a small gift, usually made of wood or straw,

on the doorstep. A small riddle was enclosed with the gift to help the recipient identify the giver.

In Sweden, Christmas Eve is a time for great celebration. Families have a festive meal, which often includes ham, meatballs, herring, and a variety of sweets. The main feast takes place on this day, usually a "Julbord" buffet, which is served at lunchtime. The "Julbord" offers a range of cold fish dishes, including various preparations of herring, gravlax (salmon cured in sugar, salt, and dill), and smoked salmon. One of the most popular desserts is "risgrynsgroet," a creamy rice pudding with a hidden almond. The person who finds the almond is said to have good luck in the coming year.

Another popular Christmas tradition in Sweden is watching classic Disney cartoons "From all of us to all of you" on Christmas Eve called "Kalle Anka och hans vaenner oenskar God Jul," at 3 p.m. which translates as "Donald Duck and his friends wish you a Merry Christmas"

One of the most beautiful and heart-warming aspects of Swedish Christmas is the "Adventsljusstake" or Advent candle holder. This is a special decoration with four candles, one of which is lit on each of the four Sundays before Christmas. Swedes also decorate their homes with traditional decorations, including simple straw and paper decorations and beautiful, hand-woven poinsettias, the "Julstjaerna."

God Jul!

Christmas Crackers and Festive Crowns

Hello! Some of the best-known traditions that make this day special are Christmas Crackers and festive paper crowns. When the family gathers around the Christmas table, each place setting includes a colorful and festive Christmas cracker. These crackers are not meant to be eaten. Before the meal begins, each person takes one end of the cracker in their hand while the closest person sitting next to them holds the other end. On the count of three, everyone winds up their crackers, making a happy "crack" sound. Inside the cracker are small toys, trinkets, or jokes that cause laughter around the table.

One of the most popular items found in Christmas cookies is a paper crown. These crowns are often colorful and decorated with glitter designs. Once the popping candy is pulled, everyone at the party puts on their paper crowns and a scene of merriment and cheer ensues.

The Christmas Cracker tradition dates back to the 19th century. It has become a popular part of British Christmas celebrations.

In the UK, traditional Christmas meals typically include roast turkey or other meats, roast potatoes, stuffing, Brussels sprouts, carrots, parsnips, gravy, and cranberry sauce, often followed by a Christmas pudding or mince pies for dessert, and festive treats like Christmas cake and mulled wine.

Sending and receiving Christmas cards to friends and family is a long-standing tradition in the UK. People in the UK can't imagine a celebration without the King's Christmas Day speech, broadcast across the nation.

We can't forget about mistletoe. Mistletoe was considered a magical plant, and the druids, the ancient priests, believed it had healing properties and brought good luck. In the Middle Ages, people began hanging mistletoe branches in their homes at Christmas time, seeing them as a symbol of love and peace. This tradition spread to other countries.

Boxing Day in the UK is a holiday on the day after Christmas (December 26). It's a time for relaxation, leftover feasts, and often, great sales in stores.

In parts of South Wales, they have the "Mari Lwyd" tradition. It involves a horse's skull adorned with ribbons on a pole, with someone hiding beneath a blanket. The horse and its crew go from house to house, playing music and singing songs. In Belfast, Northern Ireland's capital, there's the "Black Santa" tradition. The "Black Santa" collection now raises significant funds for charity each year.

Merry Christmas!

United States

Santa Claus and red stockings

Hello! Right after American families remove the extensive and intricate Halloween decorations from their homes and gardens, it's time to adorn their properties with Christmas decorations: Santas, lights, snowmen, and reindeer what makes December a month of very high electricity bills.

One of the most cherished and heartwarming customs revolves around a special treat destined for none other than Santa Claus himself. So Coca-cola, something truly American, created the Santa we know from ads, books, and decorations. An older, somewhat chubby man with a beard, a red coat, and a hat.

We all know this image spread to many other countries all over the world. As December 24 transitions from day to night, children across the country prepare for Santa's arrival. That is why they want to show him their gratitude and make his visit pleasant.

Before they go to bed, the children and their families set out a plate of freshly baked cookies and a glass of milk for Santa. The children take their role in this tradition very seriously and choose their favorite cookies

carefully and often they bake them themselves.

As children fall asleep, they imagine Santa enjoying the treats they brought him, and when they wake up on Christmas morning, the plate and jar are empty - a sign of Santa's visit. Santa Claus enters the house through the chimney and leaves presents in decorative red stockings on the mantelpiece or under the Christmas tree.

During Christmas in the USA, people enjoy a variety of delicious dishes. A popular choice is roast turkey. It is a big bird that's cooked until it's golden brown. Stuffing, made from bread, vegetables, and spices, is often prepared and the turkey is filled with it.

We can't forget about gingerbread cookies. They come in shapes like gingerbread people and houses. Decorating them with colorful icing and candy is a popular Christmas activity for whole families. Another popular dessert is pumpkin pie. People add spices and sweetness to pumpkin to make this snack delicious. Some folks add whipped cream on top for extra flavor.

During cold winter nights, Americans love to drink hot cocoa. It's a warm, chocolate beverage with marshmallows that keeps everyone feeling cozy and magical.

Merry Christmas!

Roller skating
and Hallaca

¡Hola! In Venezuela, Christmas is not just one day, but an entire festive season that begins on December 16 and lasts until January 6. During this time, you'll find fun and unique traditions that bring joy to people of all ages.

The "Hallaca" preparation is one of the most spectacular traditions. The famous Hallaca comprises sweet cornmeal with fillings such as meats, olives, or raisins. They are prepared during festivities when families get together and make them feel like an art and craft work – this time with food. The "Feria de la Chinita" begins on December 16 and starts with the Christmas festival. It is a fair where they celebrate the Virgin Mary in which they parade, play some beautiful music dance beautifully, and prepare great food. All manner of people come together for these celebrations.

People in Venezuela usually use "Gaita" for their Christmas celebration, or "Gaita zuilana." Zulia is where Gaita hails from. Some of the most popular musical genres practiced by Venezuela include "Cuatro," a four-string guitar, "Tambora," a Spanish word for drums that are peculiar to Venezuela, "Furro," a Spanish word translating into the English term for a stick drum with the capacity.

However, one of the most electrifying traditions in Venezuela is called "parrandas". These are songs about Christmas that people use to surprise their friends and neighbors. This is sort of like the musical flash mob which is full of jokes and laughter for the community.

Some do not just walk but roller skate to the church in Venezuela on Christmas Eve. This is an exciting way of getting to the "Misa de Gallo", the special Christmas Eve ceremony. Then comes the lighting of fireworks in the sky, giving way to a gift-exchanging session among family members.

In addition, two to four weeks prior to Christmas, it was common for people to paint their homes, making them attractive and ready for Christmas decoration. For Christmas and New Year's Eve, a lot of people dress in new clothes. Many people think that wearing yellow on New Year's Eve will bring them luck the following year.

Another heartwarming tradition is "El Aguinaldo." Children go from house to house, singing carols and receiving small gifts, like sweets and money. It's a joyful way for children to share the Christmas spirit.

¡Feliz Navidad!

My dream Christmas time:

Ask your parents for help with writing or draw something :)

Made in United States
Troutdale, OR
12/13/2024

26418331R00051